THE MYSTERY
OF THE
SEVERAL SEVENS

BILL BRITTAIN

THE MYSTERY
OF THE
SEVERAL SEVENS

illustrated by James Warhola

HarperCollins*Publishers*

Library of Congress Cataloging-in-Publication Data
Brittain, Bill
  The mystery of the several sevens / by Bill Brittain ; illustrated by James
Warhola.
    p.   cm.
  Summary: Mr. Merlin, a wizard disguised as a substitute teacher, magically
transports two fifth graders to a fairyland where they must solve a riddle to find
out who has stolen the seven dwarfs' bag of diamonds.
  ISBN 0-06-024459-3. — ISBN 0-06-024462-3 (lib. bdg.)
  [1. Magic—Fiction. 2. Characters and characteristics in literature—Fiction.
3. Riddles—Fiction.] I. Warhola, James, ill. II. Title.
PZ7.B78067Myp   1994   93-47076
[Fic]—dc20   CIP
                                                                            AC

Typography by Al Cetta
1   2   3   4   5   6   7   8   9   10

First Edition

—For Ginny—
After forty years, I'm still glad we
got married that day!

CONTENTS

MR. MERLIN IS BACK

"If the smile on Becky Rush's face was any bigger," I muttered to myself, "it would cut her head right in two at the mouth line."

As we walked through the big front doors of the schoolhouse, I couldn't help wondering why she was so happy. The morning was bright and clear and sparkling. Who would be happy to be in a stuffy classroom when there was baseball, and hikes, and lying on the grass watching clouds—all sorts of outside things that would be fun to do?

Then I found out the reason for Becky's smile.

"Mr. Merlin is back," she whispered in my ear. "I saw him get out of his car in the parking lot."

All of a sudden I had a smile on *my* face, too. It was just as big as Becky's. Maybe bigger.

Mr. Merlin sometimes substitutes when Ms. Dentinger, our regular fifth-grade teacher, is out.

Now Ms. Dentinger is a good teacher. She smiles a lot, and she tries to be fair, and it's fun learning from her.

But we students do get kind of tired of

hearing the same voice repeating the same things every day. We look forward to something new—something special.

Mr. Merlin is special, all right. The first time he came to our school, the class joked about how he could have been Merlin, the magician who instructed the young King Arthur centuries ago in England.

Only Becky and I found out that the "joke" was true!

The school principal, Mr. Goodman, had assigned us to kind of guide Mr. Merlin around that day. But finally, it was Mr. Merlin who guided the two of us.

During recess, when the rest of the class was outside playing, he suddenly appeared in a magician's robes and a great white beard. He took Becky and me to a king's feast at a great castle somewhere in a land beyond time. We were there almost a whole day and had grand adventures. But when we returned, the recess period—only half an hour long—was just ending.

Both Becky and I were hoping there'd be more adventures today.

We spotted Mr. Merlin at the other end of the hallway. He wore a green jacket, and his lank body and knobby knees made him look like a giant grasshopper. Snowy white hair was carefully combed over the bald spot on top of his head, and underneath his nose sprouted a huge toothbrush of a mustache.

He peered at us through black-rimmed glasses and waved. "Becky Rush and Simon Toller," he called, striding toward us. "How good to see you again."

"Are you teaching our class today?" Becky asked hopefully, as Mr. Merlin held out his hands to us.

He nodded. Our smiles got even bigger.

The three of us walked together toward

our classroom. Becky was on one side of Mr. Merlin and I was on the other.

Suddenly a fifth grader careened around a corner of the hall, running as fast as his feet, in their brand-new white sneakers, could move. He headed straight toward us.

"Stop!" Mr. Merlin cried out. "Running can be dangerous, not only for you, but for . . ."

The fifth grader didn't slow down one bit. He just stuck his tongue out at Mr. Merlin.

"Oh dear!" said the teacher with a sigh. "I guess there's nothing for it but to . . . "

As the boy scooted by us, Mr. Merlin uttered a few words in a strange language and snapped his fingers.

With a loud, frightened cry, the boy screeched to a halt, as suddenly as if he'd run into an invisible wall. Both sneakers were stuck flat against the tiles of the hallway floor. The boy struggled, but he couldn't move either foot.

"I put magic glue on the bottoms of his shoes," Mr. Merlin explained. "They won't come loose until I say so."

"Can't he just take his shoes off?" Becky asked.

"No. I covered his feet and socks with the same glue. I think fifteen minutes

there will teach him a lesson he won't soon forget."

Leaving the fifth grader anchored to the floor, we went on toward the classroom. When we entered and the rest of the students spotted Mr. Merlin, they all stopped talking and sat up a little straighter.

They'd seen Mr. Merlin in action before.

He called the roll and then glanced at Ms. Dentinger's plans for the day. "I see you start things off with a story today."

"Ms. Dentinger's stories are dumb!" mumbled Toby Rolf from a back corner. "Nothing but a bunch of sissy fairy tales."

We all wondered if Mr. Merlin was going to work some magic on Toby. But the teacher just went on calmly.

"Well, that's one opinion," he said. "How

many of you feel the same way Toby does?"

Everybody kind of looked timidly at everyone else.

"Come, come!" Mr. Merlin rapped his knuckles on the desk. "I want you all to be honest."

Slowly most of the students in the class raised their hands.

I was one of them.

So was Becky.

"A pity," murmured Mr. Merlin. "Fairy tales can be great fun. Especially if you know what *really* happened when . . . But I won't bore you with a story you

don't want to hear. Let's get on with our
first subject. Arithmetic!"

Groans were heard throughout the
classroom.

"Come on, girls and boys. Let's try this." He wrote an arithmetic problem on the front board:

$$77\sqrt{7777}$$

Silence. None of us were very good at long division.

"Seven thousand, seven hundred, seventy-seven. Who'll begin? Toby?"

No answer from the back corner.

"Doris?"

Doris Mockin bowed her head and gazed into her lap.

"Surely you know, Simon."

Mr. Merlin was pointing his finger right at me.

"Uh. . . well . . . seventy-seven goes into that first pair of sevens once."

"Excellent, so far," said Mr. Merlin.

"And there are another two sevens left,

and seventy-seven goes into them one time, so the answer is eleven!" I announced hopefully.

A frown appeared on Mr. Merlin's face. "No, Simon."

"Am I getting close?"

"In arithmetic, close doesn't count."

While Mr. Merlin and I were talking, Becky took a little battery-powered calculator from a pocket of her jeans. She punched a few buttons and then looked up.

"The answer is one-hundred and one," she said positively.

"Correct," Mr. Merlin agreed. "Now, if only we could transfer that information from your pocket to your brain, we'd be getting somewhere. However, that problem was just to get us warmed up. Today, according to Ms. Dentinger's plans, we'll be learning about roman numerals."

More groans.

"They're easy." Mr. Merlin held up one finger. With his other hand, he drew an I on the blackboard.

"Two." Two fingers. II. "Three." Three fingers. III.

"Five is V. And four is five minus one." IV.

Ten was X, and fifty was L, and a hundred was C, and five hundred was D, and a thousand was M.

"I'm never going to remember all those letters," Becky whispered across to me. "And how are you supposed to do arithmetic anyway, when you've got letters instead of numbers? This stuff just doesn't make sense."

"It does make sense, Becky," said Mr. Merlin. Those ears of his were keener than we'd thought. "In a very short time you'll see how really important roman numerals can be."

"Are we gonna have a test?" Becky asked in a worried voice.

"Yes indeed," Mr. Merlin replied. "But not your usual school test. This will be a test like none other you've ever taken."

"When is a test not a test?" I muttered, glancing at Becky.

"An interesting riddle, Simon." Mr. Merlin pointed a long, knobby finger at me. "You enjoy riddles, don't you?"

"Well . . . yeah, but . . . Hey, Mr. Merlin, I didn't mean to give you a hard time. I was just . . . "

"Perhaps we can put your fondness for puzzles to work as well, young man."

For the rest of arithmetic . . . and all of spelling . . . and science . . . Becky and I kept giving each other puzzled looks. It sounded like Mr. Merlin had something new in store for us. And we weren't sure we were going to like it.

13

Finally—recess. Everybody got to go out on the playground to yell and run around and let off a lot of steam.

Everybody? Not quite.

We started to form a line to go outside.

But suddenly, there was Mr. Merlin, staring at Becky and me.

"You two . . . stay," he told us. "You'll have more fun in here."

THE SEVEN LITTLE MEN

After taking the rest of the class outside, Mr. Merlin returned. He closed the classroom door behind him.

"Very well," he said. "Now let us begin."

With that, he extended a finger and

seemed to be drawing strange designs in the air.

The daylight outside the windows turned to dusk, then to the dark of night. *Pop!* All the overhead lights went out.

Inky blackness.

I grabbed Becky's arm.

Slowly, like the sun coming up, light returned. But the building had disappeared from around us.

We were in the middle of a forest of great, tall trees on the side of a mountain.

Mr. Merlin had changed, too. Stringy white hair fell to his shoulders, and he now had a long, snowy beard. He wore a blue robe with magical signs on it, and a pointed wizard's hat was on his head.

His black-rimmed glasses remained perched on his nose.

Becky and I still wore our school

clothes. No special costumes for us.

"Where . . . where are we?" Becky asked Mr. Merlin.

"Look about," he replied. "See if you can guess."

At first I saw nothing but the trees. Then, through an opening between two great oaks, I spotted something—no, it couldn't be.

"It . . . it looks like a gigantic shoe," I said. "But it's as big as a house."

"It *is* a house." said Mr. Merlin. "A widow lady lives there with all of her children. And I understand she treats them rather cruelly."

"'There . . . there was an old lady,'" whispered Becky, "'who lived in a shoe . . . '"

Then a sound like distant thunder came to our ears.

"That would be London Bridge, away off

yonder," Mr. Merlin told us. "It's constantly falling down, you know."

Next, to the right, I spotted a high stone tower. Near its top was a little window. A woman appeared at the window. She seemed to be removing pins or combs from hair the color of corn silk. Then she let her hair fall down the tower wall until it reached the ground.

"Rapunzel," said Mr. Merlin. "Poor thing. She's doomed to remain locked in that tower until her rescuer arrives. And he can only get in by climbing up her

hair to the window where . . . "

"The old lady in the shoe . . . London Bridge . . . Rapunzel . . . "

Becky and I stared at one another. Then we both turned to Mr. Merlin.

"Are . . . are we in fairyland?" I asked.

"Well . . . yes, you are. Now don't the two of you get angry, please. I know you think that Ms. Dentinger's stories are dumb and for sissies, but . . . "

"We're not angry," replied Becky. "We just didn't know fairyland was real. I mean . . . "

"It's as real as the king's castle I took you to last time," said Mr. Merlin. "For this is another part of that great land of imagination, where anything can come about, and a second can last forever, and a million years is but the twinkling of an eye."

"Can we go and visit the old woman's

shoe?" I asked. "Or maybe try and climb up Rapunzel's hair?"

"No time, no time," said Mr. Merlin with a shake of his head. "We have another appointment to keep."

Before Becky or I could ask any more questions, he trudged off among the trees.

For what seemed like more than an hour we followed Mr. Merlin's flapping robe through the forest. Once I heard a cackle of evil laughter from a dark cave, and a harsh voice that cried out, "Straw into gold! Straw into gold! And her firstborn shall be mine!" And Becky was sure she'd seen a white rabbit looking at its pocket watch and worrying about how late it was.

Mr. Merlin didn't stop or even slow down—he just kept striding forward, with Becky and I scurrying to keep up.

Finally we reached a log cabin, built

next to a path that ran through the tall trees. Some of the cabin's windows were round, and others were triangles. The roof was covered with thick thatch, and at one side was an old pump with a trough to hold water.

Best of all, near the front door was a wide bench. Mr. Merlin, Becky, and I all sat down to rest.

"We'll wait here for a while," said Mr. Merlin.

"Who are we waiting for?" I asked him.

"You'll see. Be patient."

The seconds and minutes passed. Then, all at once, I heard . . .

"Singing!" Becky cried out. "It sounds like men singing."

"They're coming home from work," Mr. Merlin told her.

Just then I spotted something out of the

corner of my eye. A head—a wrinkled, old man's head with a bulblike nose and large, watery eyes. Somebody was peering at us from behind a tree.

At first I thought the man was on his knees, for his head was scarcely three feet off the ground. But then the man stepped out into the clearing.

A dwarf!

Mr. Merlin got to his feet and bowed low. "My friends and I crave hospitality from you and your six brothers," he told the little man.

Six . . . and one. That was seven. Seven dwarfs!

"Hey, which one are you?" I exclaimed. "Are you Bashful or Sleepy or . . . "

"I'm neither shy nor tired, young man," replied the dwarf. "Merlin, perhaps you'd better introduce your friends."

"Simon, Becky, this is Archimedes."

Archimedes? I didn't remember any Archimedes among the seven dwarfs.

"Are your brothers with you?" Merlin asked.

"They're about. Somewhat afraid of strangers, though. I'll call them in."

Archimedes cupped his hand next to his mouth and shouted. "Einstein and Edison! Come out. Newton and Curie, you have nothing to fear! Pasteur and Salk, show yourselves!"

There was a patter of feet among the leaves on the forest floor. Other little men began to enter the clearing. All were dressed alike, in ragged pants, rough-woven shirts, thick leather shoes, and knitted caps. Their clothing, arms, and faces were grimy with dirt.

With wide eyes, Becky and I gazed at

the seven dwarfs. Their eyes were equally wide as they gazed back at us. Then, all at once, Becky began to giggle.

"Why do you laugh at us, girl?" asked the dwarf called Curie.

"Well, I . . . It's just that your names . . . "

"What about our names?" snapped Edison.

"Well . . . It seems you're all named after scientists and inventors."

"We're not named after *anybody!*" growled Salk.

"But Edison . . . Pasteur . . . Archimedes . . . "

"I suppose it never occurred to you young people," said Archimedes with a toss of his head, "that those scientists you speak of might have been named after us. I must say, Merlin, I find these young companions of yours extremely rude."

"You must excuse them," said Mr. Merlin. "It's their first time in this land. They
don't know your customs."

"Well, perhaps. But if so, you should . . ."

"By the way," Mr. Merlin went on,

"Snow White was here last time I came by. What happened to her?"

"Oh, the young princess? I thought she'd never leave. Every day when we came home from the mine, it was wash,

wash, wash, and clean, clean, clean. No time at all to relax and have fun. Thankfully, her wicked stepmother came by with that poisoned apple, or we might have been stuck with her forever."

Archimedes looked around at the other dwarfs, who were all nodding agreement.

"But no sooner do we rid ourselves of one problem than another walks in to take its place," the dwarf continued.

"What's the new problem?" Mr. Merlin asked. "Perhaps Simon and Becky and I can help you with it."

"We've been robbed."

"But Archimedes," said Mr. Merlin, "if someone came along while you were away at work and took a bowl or a chair or something like that, you can surely replace it without much trouble."

"It was more than a bowl or a chair,

Merlin. This is serious, I tell you."

"You mean . . . "

Archimedes nodded. "Yes. Yesterday, while we were off digging in our mine, someone stole a whole bag—nearly ten pounds—of our largest and most brilliant diamonds!"

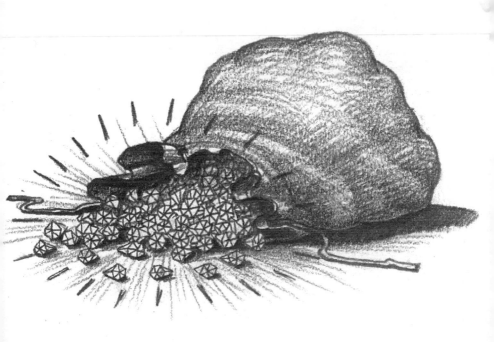

SEVEN SUSPECTS

"As you know, Merlin, we don't dig those diamonds out of the earth just for the fun of it."

We were all in the log cabin, sitting at a table of rough-hewn planks and listening to Archimedes, who seemed to be the leader of the seven little men.

"Then what *do* you do with the diamonds," I asked, "after you've found them?"

"We keep them in the store room, out back," was the reply. "Then, every six weeks or so, Old King Cole sends a squad of knights to take them to the palace. It's the rent we pay so that the king will allow us to live here in peace."

Becky and I kept trying to imagine how much ten pounds of diamonds would be worth in our world. "What does King Cole do with so many gems?" she asked.

"His queen takes most of them," said Pasteur, "for jewelry and crowns and such. The knights and soldiers mount them on the hilts of their swords, and the royal bloodhounds wear diamond-studded collars. Oh, and the young prince got a bag of diamond marbles for his last birthday."

"In a few days, King Cole will be expecting his diamonds from us," murmured Archimedes ominously. "But we will have none to give him. Oh, how angry he will be."

"Can't you just explain what happened?" I asked.

"When it comes to collecting his rents," chirped Einstein in a high voice, "the king accepts no excuses. He may even want to behead us. He has a fearful temper. Whoever wrote that poem about Old King Cole being a 'merry old soul' was either a liar or a fool."

"Then it's clear there's only one thing to be done," said Mr. Merlin. "We have to find out who stole the diamonds before the king's knights come for the rent."

"But . . . but how's that to be accomplished?" asked Archimedes.

Mr. Merlin looked to his right, where

Becky was sitting, and then to his left at me. A little smile passed across his lips.

"Becky, Simon, how do you think we should begin?"

We both thought for a moment. "This cabin is way off in the woods," said Becky finally. "There can't be too many people who go by and guess that you store diamonds here."

"That is true," Archimedes replied. All the other dwarfs nodded solemnly in agreement.

"Think," Becky went on. "We need the names of anyone who comes by here regularly. One of them *has* to be the thief."

There was much *hmmming* and *ahhing* and head-scratching as the dwarfs tried to remember. Becky leaned toward me. "You'd better take notes, Simon," she told me.

I pulled my assignment book and a

pencil from my shirt pocket and got ready to write.

"Michael comes to the forest one day a week, searching out wood for his wagons," said Salk finally.

"And Henry comes, too," added Edison. "He needs good cedar for the barrels he makes."

"Samuel's often riding by in his wagon, looking for horses to shoe," put in Curie.

"Oh!" Suddenly Newton sat up straight in his chair. "Just the other day, Arthur waved to me as we passed each other on the trail."

"And don't forget about James," chirped Einstein. "He's constantly crisscrossing the forest paths."

"Oftentimes I've watched Benjamin paddle his boat down the creek yonder," put in Pasteur timidly.

"And it's no secret that Richard comes

to the forest to look for the straightest of branches for the arrows he fashions," said Archimedes with a nod of his head.

"Michael . . . Henry . . . Samuel . . . Arthur . . . James . . . Benjamin . . . Richard." I pronounced each name as I scrawled it onto a page of my notebook. "Anybody else?"

The dwarfs looked at one another. Then they all stared at me. Seven heads shook back and forth as if tied together with string.

"That's a start," Becky said. "But you only gave us the first names of all these guys. Don't they have any last names?"

The dwarfs looked at one another in confusion. "What's a . . . a 'last name'?" Archimedes asked.

"It's . . . like . . . your parents' name," I said. "And it sets you apart from anyone else with the same first name."

"But there's only one Richard hereabouts," Archimedes told me.

"Suppose another Richard came along?" I asked in exasperation.

"Then we could identify ours in a number of ways. His work is one of them. Richard, you see, makes arrows. Such a person is called a fletcher. So our man would be Richard-the-Fletcher."

"Henry's a cooper," said Edison. "He makes barrels. Therefore, Henry-the-Cooper."

"And our Samuel, who works with iron . . . Samuel-the-Smith," added Curie.

"Don't forget our wagon maker," yipped Salk. "Michael-the-Wainwright."

"A man's work isn't the only way he can be known," Archimedes told me. "There's the place where he lives, for example."

"Since Arthur lives away down the valley, we sometimes speak of Arthur-of-the-

Glen," said Newton.

"Then there's James-of-the-Hill," Einstein piped up.

"And Benjamin-of-the-Rivers," added Pasteur with a gap-toothed smile.

As the dwarfs talked, I was writing names as fast as I could. Leaving out all the in-between words, I finally had the list of suspects:

Arthur Glen
Benjamin Rivers
Henry Cooper
James Hill
Michael Wainwright
Richard Fletcher
Samuel Smith

"Seven suspects." I glanced over at Mr. Merlin. "You really are landing on that number seven today, aren't you?"

"We've scarcely begun," he replied with a grin.

"Okay." Becky was all business. "Now we know one of these seven guys stole the diamonds. The question is, which one?"

"How can we determine that?" asked Archimedes. "All seven of us dwarfs were digging away at our diamond mine when the bag was stolen."

"Oh, there must be a way," said Mr. Merlin, twirling a finger into his white beard. "Think carefully."

With more head-scratching and groaning, the dwarfs set to thinking.

Then Einstein slammed his hand against the tabletop. "Of course!" he cried out.

"Of course what?" growled Archimedes.

"Walpurgia—she'd know. She's always snooping in that crystal ball of hers, trying to find out what everybody else is doing. I'll bet she was looking into the glass and saw who stole the diamonds. We can just send someone over to ask her . . . "

"But Walpurgia is a . . . a witch!" Einstein almost screamed. "Who'd dare go and see her about anything?"

Archimedes looked about at the other dwarfs. "Are there any volunteers?" he asked.

All the dwarfs shook their heads. They'd rather take their chances with an angry King Cole than with Walpurgia the Witch.

"Nobody wants to risk getting Walpurgia angry at them," Archimedes finally announced.

"Don't worry about it," said Becky bravely. "If this Walpurgia is the only one who can help, I'll see that we get the right information from her."

"Are . . . are you going to her house?"

asked Curie timidly.

"Nope. I'm sending my assistant."

It took me a couple of seconds to realize that Becky was talking about *me*!

"Hey, Becky!" I shouted. "Who put you in charge?"

"Somebody's got to be the boss. And I'm it. Get ready, Simon. You're going to the witch's house."

"But I don't wanna . . . "

"Hey, last time we went out with Mr. Merlin, it was me that fought the monster, wasn't it? Well, I'm not going to do all the dirty work. This time it's your turn."

Before I could protest any more, all the dwarfs began cheering. Salk and Newton began pounding me on the back and telling me how brave I was.

What was a guy going to do?

I was going to see Walpurgia the Witch, that's what.

WALPURGIA

All during the long, lonely walk along the
path to the witch's house, I kept thinking of
the advice the dwarfs had given me.

"Don't look deeply into Walpurgia's
eyes. She might hypnotize you."

"Don't be nibbling at the walls and
windows, no matter how tempting they

may look."

"And above all, don't, under any circumstances, allow Walpurgia to lure you inside! That would put you in her power, and she'll capture you for sure!"

Finally I rounded a turn in the path, and there was the house. It wasn't hard to recognize, for the dwarfs had described it in detail.

Its walls were of gingerbread, and the roof was made of big slabs of chocolate cake with thick frosting. Candy and cookies decorated the walls, and the windowpanes were of transparent melted sugar.

Then I remembered the tale of *Hansel and Gretel* that Mom used to read to me when I was little.

This was the same witch's house—I was sure of it.

I was so surprised by my discovery that I didn't hear a window being raised from inside. But suddenly a harsh, cackling voice came to my ears.

"Getting a little hungry, are you, boy?"

There, leaning on the windowsill and looking out at

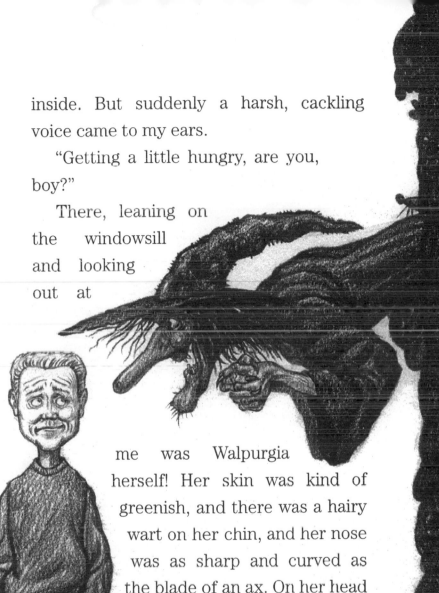

me was Walpurgia herself! Her skin was kind of greenish, and there was a hairy wart on her chin, and her nose was as sharp and curved as the blade of an ax. On her head was a high, pointed hat with a wide brim. She stared at me, and her eyes glittered ominously.

"Don't look deeply into Walpurgia's eyes."

I bowed my head and looked down at my shoes.

"You look famished, boy," she told me. "Have a nibble from the wall. Just there, where that lovely candy cane hangs."

"Don't be nibbling at the walls and windows."

"No ma'am, I'd rather not," I said, shaking my head. "I just came to ask a question."

"A question? Oh, I do love riddles. What is your question, lad?"

"In your crystal ball, did you see the man who stole the diamonds from the seven dwarfs?"

Walpurgia thought about this for a moment. "Yes," she told me finally. "Yes, I believe I did. Just a moment."

The window slammed shut. A moment later the door opened. "The picture of the burglary is still within my crystal ball," announced Walpurgia with a nasty laugh. "Just step in here, and we can both watch it on instant replay."

I walked to the door. Walpurgia beckoned to me.

I went into the house. As I stood looking about at the huge iron pot on the fireplace and the shelves of jars and cans, and the books of spells and magic, I heard in my mind the voice of the dwarf Archimedes, just as if he'd been standing beside me:

"Don't, under any circumstances, allow Walpurgia to lure you inside!"

Click!

I turned to dash outside. "Too late, boy," I heard the witch cackle.

She was kneeling beside me. Her hands were still on the iron band she'd locked around my ankle. The band was attached to one end of a thick chain. The chain's other end was firmly fastened to the inner wall of the house.

"You're my prisoner, boy," she announced.

I remembered what had almost happened to Hansel in the story. "Are . . . are you going to cook me in the stove and make a meal of me?" I asked.

"Of course not," Walpurgia said. "You'll just stay here and be my slave and wait on me hand and foot. Oh, what fun we'll have."

It didn't sound much like fun to me. I wanted to be back at school, where I belonged.

"Let's play riddles," the witch went on. "A face that neither smiles nor frowns, and two hands that never clap. What is it?"

"That's easy," I said glumly, rattling my

chain. "A clock."

"You think you're pretty smart, don't you?" she grumbled. "Well, try this one. How do you get down off an elephant?"

"You don't get down off an elephant." Was I going to have to spend the rest of my life chained to a wall and answering these silly riddles? "You get down off a duck."

"Arrr!" Walpurgia snarled. "I'll bet you think you know everything, boy. Well, what's the longest word in your language?"

I'd never thought about that. Could it be *halitosis*? Or *psychiatric*, maybe?

"You don't know, do you?" screeched Walpurgia in triumph.

I shook my head.

"You see—you're not so smart. The word is smiles."

"*Smiles?* But that isn't very long."

"It is, too. It's a mile between the two s's. Ha, ha. Got you!"

"I don't want to play riddles anymore," I told the witch.

"But you have to. You're my slave."

"I don't care. I'm through answering those dumb questions."

"Just one more?"

"No!"

Walpurgia looked at me and pouted. It was clear she loved her riddles. "Tell you what," she said finally. "Let me give you one more riddle. If you answer it, I'll let you go free. *And* I'll tell you who stole the dwarfs' diamonds."

"Okay," I told her. "It's a deal. What's the riddle?"

"You have nine coins. They all look the same, and they all weigh the same—except for one. That one coin is just a teensy bit heavier, though you can't tell just by holding it in your hand. And you also have a scale—the kind with pans that hang from a balance arm."

"Okay," I said. "I understand so far."

"Good. Now you must pick out the heaviest coin . . . "

"That's easy. You just keep weighing until . . . "

" . . . but you only get to use the scale two times," the witch finished with a leer.

Two times? The thing was impossible. I mean, you had nine coins. That wasn't an even number. But if you put four coins on one side and five on the other, then . . . Nope, try again. Four on one side and four on the other?

I was getting nowhere, really fast. Three on one side, and three on the other? But what about . . . ?

Then, all at once, I had it! "Here's the way it works," I said triumphantly. "First weighing: you put three coins on one pan, and three on the other. Now either one pan tips down, or both pans stay even."

"Let's say one pan goes down," mumbled Walpurgia with a mean look in her eye.

"Then we know that pan has the heavy coin. In any case, now we know the heavy coin is one of a group of three."

"But you only have one more weighing, you young scut!"

"So I take two of the coins—any two of the three—and place one in each pan."

"This time, we'll pretend the pans stay even. What then, slave boy?"

"Then we know the heavy coin is the one that wasn't weighed."

"Oh!" In a rage, Walpurgia hopped about the room. "How I hate it when my best riddles get answered. Hate! Hate! Hate!"

"But now you have to release me," I said. "You promised, Walpurgia."

"But I'm a witch. So I don't have to keep my promises. And if I keep you chained up here, who'll be the wiser? No, young fool. You shall stay . . ."

Boom!

Suddenly the thick door of the house exploded into the room. Walpurgia was almost knocked off her feet as the door crashed against the far wall.

There in the doorway, outlined by the

bright sunlight behind him, stood Mr. Merlin. A great wind billowed his magic robe about him. Slowly he raised one arm. He pointed an accusing finger straight at the witch.

"You promised!" he roared in a deep voice that shook the very stones on which the candy house was built.

"But Merlin," gasped the witch as her lower lip quivered with fright, "sometimes we witches do not . . ."

"You promised!"

"If I could only make you . . ."

"You promised!"

"Oh, very well, blast you!"
Walpurgia waved both hands toward my chained ankle. *Pop!*

The iron band opened. I was
free!

"Now go. Get out of here. Both of
you." She made a brushing gesture
toward the open doorway, as if Mr.
Merlin and I were dust that she was
sweeping away.

"Not yet, I think," Mr. Merlin told her. "For you promised Simon another thing."

"Oh? D'you mean you're still worried about who stole the diamonds from the dwarfs? All right . . . here!"

Walpurgia waved her right hand in a large circle. Suddenly there was something in it.

A piece of paper, folded and sealed with wax.

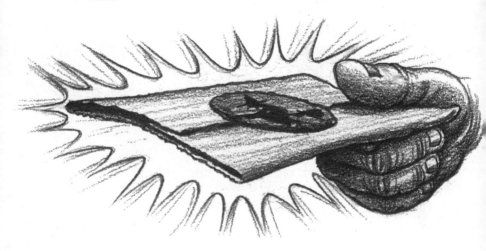

"On this is written the identity of the thief," said the witch. "But you must not break the wax seal until you arc back at the cabin of the dwarfs."

"How do I know you're not trying to trick me again, Walpurgia?" I asked.

"Because I pledge my witchly honor to the truth of what I have said," she replied.

"I dunno, Mr. Merlin. If she cheats . . . "

"She has pledged her witchly honor," he replied. "Therefore, she cannot lie to us. The paper gives us the name of the guilty person."

"Then can we leave? Right now?"

"Of course, Simon. Whenever you wish."

"And don't ever return and try to find me," said the witch in a raspy voice, "as I intend to make myself invisible to you forever."

With that, Mr. Merlin and I left the house of Walpurgia. As she stood in the doorway watching us go, I thought I glimpsed a crafty gleam in her eye. But I figured I was just imagining things.

Mr. Merlin and I took the trail that led to the dwarfs' cabin. In my right hand was clutched the folded piece of paper, held closed by a seal of wax.

EVEN MORE SEVENS

When we got back to the dwarfs' cabin,
I told everybody all about how I'd been
captured by Walpurgia and made to answer
the riddles, and how Mr. Merlin had finally
rescued me.

Okay, I didn't tell everything. I never

said a word about how scared I'd been.

Finally I held up the folded paper triumphantly. "And here's the name of the person who stole your diamonds," I said.

"Tell us who it is," squeaked Einstein. "We'll drag the scoundrel back here and—"

"All we have to do," Archimedes interrupted, "is give the name to King Cole. He'll take care of the punishment. The king is never merrier than when he has a criminal to punish."

"But Archimedes, wouldn't it be fun for us to . . . "

"How about if we have a lot less talk and a little more action," snapped Becky impatiently. "So far we don't even know who the guilty party is. Here, Simon, give me the paper. I want to see the criminal's name."

Before I could protest, Becky snatched the paper from my hand. With a fingernail, she broke open the wax seal. Then she unfolded the paper and looked at it.

She looked at it for a long time.

Too long.

"Well, maybe that witch gave you the name," she said finally. "But I sure can't find it here."

"Let me see that thing." Archimedes snatched the paper from Becky and read what was on it. "Oh, dear. Oh, dear," he moaned. "We may never know."

"Walpurgia *had* to give us the name," said Mr. Merlin. "She promised on her witchly honor. Archimedes, put the paper on the table where we can all see it."

The dwarf put Walpurgia's note on the rough planks. We all bent over it.

Instead of a name, there were four lines of writing near the top of the page, and a fifth scrawled near the bottom.

The four top lines made a kind of poem:

Put Emma's figures sevenfold
 The seven seas come next, be told.
Then seven times to end this rhyme.
 All turned about will solve the crime.

"Not fair! Not fair!" chanted Edison. "Walpurgia promised to give us a name, and she didn't do it. Not fair!"

"I think you're wrong," said Mr. Merlin. "In her own way, Walpurgia has been very fair."

"What do you mean, Mr. Merlin?" I asked. "She didn't tell . . . "

"But she did. Walpurgia loves riddles and word games. That poem is a clue to the name we're searching for. Now it's up to us to find it."

"Us?" said Becky. "I think it's up to me.

Look at that line at the bottom of the page."

We all read the cramped, handwritten line together:

Work this out on your machine, girl!

"I'm the only girl here," Becky continued. "And the only machine I have is my little calculator. So my guess is this is an arithmetic problem of some kind."

"First seven dwarfs, and then seven suspects," I moaned. "And now some kind of figures sevenfold, and seven seas and seven times . . . times something."

"Don't forget," Becky added, "that back in school, you didn't know how much seven thousand, seven hundred seventy-seven divided by seventy-seven was. There are some more sevens for you."

"Sevens wherever we look" I said. "How are we even going to . . . "

"We work at it, Simon." Becky took her calculator out of her pocket. She punched the 7 button and then tapped it again. "Well, at least we know seven times seven is still forty-nine."

"Yeah, but the poem talks about 'Emma's figures.' Who's Emma?"

"I dunno. That's one thing we've got to figure out."

"And seven seas? Let's see. The Atlantic Ocean, the Pacific Ocean, the . . . "

"The oceans? I don't think so." Becky shook her head. "The seven seas are something else. I'm sure of it."

"But what?"

"It's a riddle, Simon. We have to think about it."

"What I'm thinking is that Walpurgia

just wrote down some nonsense. And she's having a good laugh at us for taking it seriously."

"No. Don't forget what Mr. Merlin said about witchly honor. Walpurgia had to give the right answer, even if it's in riddle form. Hey, I've got an idea."

"What?" I muttered glumly.

"Tell me the riddles Walpurgia asked while you were chained up in her house. Maybe there'll be a hint in one of them."

"Well, first she asked me what had a face that neither smiles nor frowns, and two hands that never clap. It was a clock, of course."

"Face . . . " Becky patted her cheek. "It can be the face of a human, or a clock's dial. Two meanings. Hmmm."

"Then Walpurgia wanted to know how you got down off an elephant. I told her you couldn't get down off an elephant. You got down off a duck."

"Down. It could mean toward the ground, and it could mean a duck's feathers. Another word with more than one meaning. Hmmm and more hmmm."

"The next riddle was to give the longest word in English. She said it was *smiles* because there was *mile* between the two *s*'s."

"Smiles . . . ha! It has the *sound* of mile in it, even if the word has nothing to do with distance. Better and better. Sounds are the important things. We're really getting somewhere, Simon."

"Maybe you think so, Becky. But I don't."

"But there's still something I . . . Yes, that's got to be it. Where's Mr. Merlin?"

"He went outside someplace. Why?"

"Doesn't it seem strange to you that he

isn't here helping us?"

"Gee, I don't know."

"Listen, Simon. Back in class, we said we didn't think much of Ms. Dentinger's fairy tales. So Mr. Merlin brought us to this . . . this fairyland. Then you couldn't say how much is seven thousand, seven hundred seventy-seven divided by seventy-seven. Now we've got more sevens than we know what to do with. Don't you see what's going on?"

"No."

"This poem isn't the witch's doing. It's really Mr. Merlin, testing us—just as he said he would."

"C'mon, Becky. When Mr. Merlin mentioned the test, he was talking about roman numerals."

"Roman numerals . . ." Becky stared hard at the paper. "Words that mean more than one thing . . . sounds . . . "

Suddenly her eyes got round and wide. "Yes!" she cried out loudly. "Oh yes! Oh yes! Oh yes!"

She was on to something. Boy, I felt stupid.

"I need a pencil, Simon," she ordered.

I looked about the room. No desk, no paper, no pencils. Those dwarfs didn't need . . .

"Check your pocket, dummy," Becky barked.

I took out the pencil and handed it to her. She turned the paper over and began scribbling words. Every now and then she'd peek at Walpurgia's poem. Then she'd begin writing again.

I stood it about as long as I could. "What are you writing?" I asked finally.

She finished a final few words. "Here it is," she said. "Listen."

"I don't want to listen. I want to see it for myself."

"No fair. You've got to *hear* this first."

"Okay. But then can I read it?"

"Then I'll *make* your read. But first . . . "

Becky began reading, and I listened as carefully as if she was giving me my first driving lesson.

When she finished, she looked straight into my eyes. "Was that the poem you saw on the paper?" she asked.

"It sure was. Oh, you didn't pronounce 'Emma' quite right. But the rest was just like . . . "

"No, it wasn't!" she practically crowed. "It was a lot different. Take a look at what I wrote."

She handed me the paper. I read the words Becky had set down in her neat script. They were the same. Only . . . only . . .

They were different, too.

THE SEVEN SOLUTION

Put M as figures sevenfold.
  The seven C's come next, be told.
Then seven times two end this rhyme.
  All turned about will solve the crime.

"You're right," I told Becky. "Your poem

sounds almost exactly like the one Walpurgia gave me. But you have changed some of it."

"I think this is what the witch was really saying," Becky said. "The other words she put in were just to make it into a riddle."

"It's still a riddle as far as I'm concerned. Your poem is just as puzzling as the other one."

"No it isn't, Simon. Remember how everything that's happened to us here goes back to what we were talking about in school?"

"Yeah, but . . ."

"Well, in school, we were talking about roman numerals. And roman numerals look like letters."

"You mean the letters in the poem are . . ."

"Exactly! So if we put M into figures,

the way the first line says . . . "

"Hey, in roman numerals, M is a thousand."

"Right. But we need that figure 'sevenfold'—or seven times. So . . . "

Becky took her little calculator from her pocket. I heard a clicking sound as she punched the keys. The last key she hit was the plus sign. A figure appeared in the display window.

7000

"Next comes 'The seven C's'", I said.

"And in roman numerals, C is one hundred."

Click, click, click . . . click. Another number appeared in the window.

700

"Okay, Becky. Now in the third line,

Walpurgia wrote 'Then seven times to end this rhyme.' You changed it so it's seven times two.'"

"They sound alike. And seven times two is . . ."

Click, click . . . click.

In the window appeared.

14

"But why did you press the plus sign when you entered each number?" I asked Becky. "How do you know you're supposed to add?"

"The last line begins with the word *all*," she answered. "I think that means the numbers are supposed to be added up."

With that—*click*—she pressed the calculator's equal sign button.

7714

I looked at the answer. "Seven thousand, seven hundred and fourteen," I murmured. "Well, we've got a couple more sevens to complicate things. And I'm just as mystified as ever."

"So am I," Becky agreed. "But according to the poem, whatever we get has to be turned about. Let's try it."

She cleared the calculator screen and punched keys.

Click, click, click, click.

५।ㄱㄱ

I took the calculator from Becky and stared at it. The answer was turned about all right. "Four thousand, one hundred and seventy-seven. Big deal. Where does that get us?"

"I don't know," she said, giving me a shamefaced look. "I can't figure out what to do next. It . . . it's still just so much nonsense."

Nonsense—that seemed like a good word for what we were doing. Idly I entered the numbers from the poem.

$$7000$$

Then:

$$700$$

And:

$$14$$

I pressed the equal sign button. "Dumb!" I cried out. "The whole thing is dumb. How can Mr. Merlin expect us to . . . "

Then I realized that Becky wasn't paying any attention to me.

She was staring at the calculator in my hand.

"That's it!" she whispered breathlessly.

"What's it, Becky?"

"Simon, get out your list of suspects and take a good look at it."

I pulled out my notebook and turned pages. There was the list:

> *Arthur Glen*
> *Benjamin Rivers*
> *Henry Cooper*
> *James Hill*
> *Michael Wainwright*
> *Richard Fletcher*
> *Samuel Smith*

"Now see what the calculator says," Becky continued.

But before I could glance down, Becky had plucked it out of my hand. "'All turned about,' as the poem says," she told me.

With that, Becky turned the calculator around so that the top of the screen was toward me.

And there, printed out clearly on the screen, was the name of the thief who'd stolen the dwarfs' diamonds:

hILL

"James Hill," I sputtered. "He's the one who . . ."

Before I could say any more, the seven dwarfs came rushing into the cabin. Behind them was Mr. Merlin, his robe fluttering like a great blue flag.

"We heard, we heard!" shouted Archimedes. "Now Old King Cole will know we're not responsible for the loss of the diamonds."

"But what will happen to James Hill?" Becky asked.

"He'll be sentenced to hard labor at the palace," replied Edison. "Making the beds and polishing the shoes of all the ladies in waiting and picking up after all the knights and soldiers. Oh, it'll be horrible!"

"Thank you both!" exclaimed Pasteur. "Thank you for discovering who the thief was."

"Oh, it was nothing," said Becky, grinning. "But I was rather good, wasn't I?"

"Hey, wait a minute," I protested. "Your part was easy. If I hadn't been brave enough to go to the witch's house and make her give me that paper . . . "

"It was Mr. Merlin who made Walpurgia give us the poem, and you know it, Simon. Besides, only a real dope would get himself chained up the way you did. I was the one who . . . "

"Have done, have done, the both of you," said Mr. Merlin, chuckling to himself. "You needed each other to solve this mystery. And I think you both performed splendidly."

Then he turned to the dwarfs. "Our

time here in your land is done," Mr. Merlin told them. "We must return whence we came."

"We understand," Archimedes answered. "But come again, and visit us whenever you can. You—and your young friends—will always find a welcome at our cabin."

Mr. Merlin began drawing odd designs in the air with his hands. The inside of the cabin grew dark.

When the light came up again, we were back in our schoolroom. Mr. Merlin had on the same jacket and pants he was wearing when we'd first seen him in the hall that morning.

"We must have spent most of the day with dwarfs," I said.

"Remember what I told you," Mr. Merlin replied. "In the land of imagination, a second can last forever, and a million years is but the twinkling of an eye."

From outside came the shouts of the boys and girls on the playground. I saw our class lining up to come into the building.

"Half an hour," I murmured, finding it hard to believe. "The whole thing . . . the dwarfs . . . Walpurgia . . . all of it. Only half an hour."

"Where . . . where will you take us next time, Mr. Merlin?" asked Becky.

Mr. Merlin didn't reply.

He just looked at the two of us.

Smiled.

And winked his eye.

BILL BRITTAIN's tales of the rural New England village of Coven Tree are well loved by children of all ages. *The Wish Giver* was a 1984 Newbery Honor Book; it and *Devil's Donkey* were both named ALA Notable Children's Books as well as *School Library Journal* Best Books. The third Coven Tree novel, *Dr. Dredd's Wagon of Wonders*, was a 1988 Children's Editors' Choice (ALA *Booklist*), and the fourth, *Professor Popkin's Prodigious Polish*, was named a "Pick of the Lists" by *American Bookseller*.

Mr. Brittain has written many other delightful books, including *All the Money in the World* which won the 1982–1983 Charlie May Simon Children's Book Award and was adapted for television as an ABC-TV Saturday Special. He is also the author of two fast-paced mysteries, *Who Knew There'd Be Ghosts?*, a Children's Choice for 1986 (IRA/CBC), and its sequel, *The Ghost From Beneath the Sea*. His most recent book for HarperCollins is *Shape-Changer*, a tale of eerie suspense.

Bill Brittain lives with his wife, Ginny, in Asheville, North Carolina.

JAMES WARHOLA has illustrated a number of children's books, including *Hurricane City* by Sarah Weeks. He lives in Kingston, New York.